BREAKING

THE SILENCE ON
GENDER MATTERS IN THE CHURCH

STANLEY MAPHOSA© 2020

Foreword by Pastor Xana McCauley: Rhema
Bible Church North

Printed in South Africa

First Printing, 2020

ISBN 978-0-6398026-0-2

Published by S3R Consulting

Roodepoort

South Africa 1724

www.s3rconsulting.co.za

TABLE OF CONTENTS

DEDICATION

The purpose of this book is to serve churches by addressing difficult issues that can prevent women and girl children from experiencing 'life in all its fullness' *(John 10:10)*. Some of these issues are related to harmful gender-related perceptions, attitudes and actions.

This book is dedicated to all who have an interest in seeing women and girls fulfil their God-given destinies.

I would like to thank the one true God – Father, Son and Holy Spirit – for the gift of writing and the power to believe in my passion and pursue my dreams. I could never have done it without the faith I have in you, the Almighty.

To my wife Soneni, I am so thankful that I have you in my corner, pushing me when I am ready to give up. All the good that comes from this book I look forward to sharing with you! You are my Buddy and my Hero. Thanks for not just believing but knowing that I could do it again – I love you now and forever. To my

children, Shekinah Mayibongwe and Rejoice Nozuko; you
are   my   best

achievement in life. You welcomed me into fatherhood, and I am grateful for you.

To my parents, Bishop Meja Engelbert and Pastor Isabel Maphosa: thank you for the wisdom, love and support you have given me. To my siblings, in-laws, cousins, friends, and work colleagues, past and present, you are my biggest fans and for that I am grateful.

I would like to express my appreciation of my editors, my designers, marketers, promoters, and publishers. I love you more than you will ever know.

FOREWORD

Pastor Xana McCauley: Rhema Bible Church North

It's 2018 and the world at large has a bias against gender equality. Our cultures and attitudes have been shaped by ideas of inequality which permeate many spheres of life. These harmful perceptions rob people of their dignity as human beings.

Sadly, many churches have absorbed this bias, often unaware of the disconnect between culture and God's plan for humanity. A theology of inequality that promotes harm and restricts God's blueprint for the church has been developed and embraced. Our slanted teachings in the church have a negative effect on our families, our daily lives, and our witness.

Stanley Maphosa's book is a much-needed resource for the church today. While staying true to biblical scriptures, he unpacks their context, the meaning of words written in their original language, and in so doing, enlightens the reader on God's

purposes for all human beings. It is only by believing
that   God

distributes gifts to all by the Holy Spirit *(1 Corinthians 12:11),* regardless of gender, that the church will be in a position to display God's original plan of creation.

I recommend this book for your prayerful reflection. Let the church lead the way and display God to the world. Let it be known that God neither shows partiality nor discriminates according to gender.

I leave you with this prayer: "I pray that the eyes of your heart will have enough light to see what the hope of God's call is, what is the richness of God's glorious inheritance among believers." *(Ephesians 1:18 CEV)*

INTRODUCTION

I first heard of female emancipation when the United Nations organised the fourth World Conference on Women in Beijing in 1995, which led to the Beijing Platform of Action, from which resulted various protocols, frameworks and legislation promoting the development of women. After that historic conference, some women wanted overnight change, while men tended to misinterpret the outcomes of the conference and the radical activism of the feminists. The point needs to be made that feminism is a movement, but gender equality and equity are day to day matters that everyone needs to understand and always approach with great sensitivity.

The Beijing Conference's fifth Sustainable Development Goal calls for 'achieving gender equality and empowering all women and girls by 2030'. This is a tall order as it envisages the empowerment of all women and girls within a specific timeframe.

This involves four areas of empowerment: legal, political, socio-economic, and spiritual. Legal empowerment means having the right laws, policies and institutions in place to ensure that the rights of women are upheld and protected. Consequences for violence against women and children should be serious and serve as a deterrent. Political empowerment means making sure we have women representatives in government and in decision-making positions in other organisations. Socio-economic empowerment will ensure that women have access to tools that will enable them to play an active role in socio-economic development. A lot has been achieved in these three areas, but much more still needs to be done.

This book addresses the spiritual empowerment of women. We discuss what has been done, why and how it has been done. We also look at what has not been done and make suggestions about what should be done. The Christian response to gender matters should be grounded in and motivated by the word of God. As followers of Christ we are God's representatives (WHO we are) and we respond to God's calling us as His children (WHAT we are called to do).This book is a guide for deep thinking and reflection on gender matters in the church, now and in the future.

There are ten guiding principles based on scripture, which I trust will help us in our journey towards equity and equality for all as believers in Christ.

Genesis begins by telling us about our Creator and our creation. A crucial message in Genesis is that male and female were created together in God's image and as stewards, indicating that men and women share a common origin and responsibility. Every person's value and significance is derived from that basic truth. The truth of our creation by God in His image influences how we act towards one another. Our attitudes and all our relationships and actions should acknowledge the value of both male and female in God's sight. We need to be considerate towards all people, keep their well-being in mind, and demonstrate compassion when someone's dignity has been disregarded, stripped from them or damaged in any way. Our motivation and model should come from the example of Jesus Christ as portrayed in the gospels.

In the Old Testament, the word 'shalom' encompassed completeness, wholeness, well-being, vitality, fulfilment and healthy relationships. Shalom describes the well-being of a community where justice and righteousness prevail.

In his book, Not the Way it's Supposed to be: A Breviary of Sin Cornelius Plantinga comments:

In the Bible, shalom means universal flourishing, wholeness and delight – a rich state of affairs in which natural needs are satisfied and natural gifts fruitfully employed, a state of affairs that inspires joyful wonder as its Creator and Saviour opens doors and welcomes the creatures in whom he delights. Shalom, in other words, is the way things ought to be.

In the New Testament the Kingdom of God embodies shalom. The Christians' living hope motivates them to work towards God's shalom and kingdom in their families and communities. We can therefore reach towards wholeness and work towards mutual fulfilment, well-being and healthy relationships. Together we can grow and become the mature persons God created us to be.

Our Christian response to gender matters needs to be practical rather than emotional. We need to cross the barriers of our comfort zones and take steps to demonstrate the accepting love of Christ towards all people, irrespective of their gender. Jesus reached out to all the women He met and embraced

them with loving care. We likewise need to accept all
men   and

women in Christ as our brothers and sisters. Jesus showed God's mercy and called His disciples to be merciful. In a patriarchal society where, male religious leaders were authoritative, Jesus opposed attitudes which degraded women while restoring their dignity, and we therefore need to oppose negative behaviour towards women – especially gender-based violence.   In the first congregations in the book of Acts, women played important roles in spite of the prevailing patriarchal culture of the time. Balanced participation in leadership by both female and male will be more just and will benefit both the church and communities in general.

It is important that we grapple humbly with these difficult gender issues with wisdom that comes from the Holy Spirit, and we must communicate the truth, but always with sensitivity and love. When we stand against those who are in breach of the rights of the vulnerable people, we need love and courage, because we stand up for justice. When we do this, through our prayers, advocacy and challenging leaders, we follow the example of prophets and priests from Old Testament times.

I pray that you will enjoy reading about and reflecting on the various aspects of our calling to ensure that the body of Christ is healthy, and that families will grow in their understanding of God's call to us to take responsibility for our spiritual and physical health. S3R Consulting is available for discussions, training and speaking engagements on these critical matters.

The Lord bless all who read and study this work and may more people understand God's call to action in relation to gender.

Stanley Maphosa

CHAPTER 1: Men and women were together created in God's image as God's representatives

Biblical texts:

Genesis 1:26-28, 31, 2:18-25; Luke 24:1-10; Acts 2:16-18; 2 Corinthians 3:17-18; Ephesians 4:15-16, 22-24

Introduction

We live in a patriarchal society that favours men – at home, at work and in the community. The advantages that men have over women, especially in the fields of study and career advancement cannot be overemphasised. While the ratio of boys to girls is generally evenly balanced when they start school, this changes in later years, with girl child dropouts due to such factors as pregnancy, early marriage, and even, in some families, a preference to educate boys rather than girls.

Bible narratives help us understand our own stories and create new ones that demonstrate God's love and grace. Reading the story of creation slowly and prayerfully sheds light on relationships between men and women in our churches and community today. The Bible teaches the equality of men and women in creation and in redemption. This means something went wrong between creation and redemption which we must make right.

Key biblical reflection points

1. Read **Genesis 1:26-28, 31.** How does the knowledge that God created humankind in this way make you feel about being a man or a woman? Do you think these verses have a different message for men than for women? What are the implications for the way we look at each other and how we act towards each other as men and women?

2. Read **Genesis 2:18-23.** This story has been used by men to claim that they are superior to women. Why is this a wrong interpretation of the passage? Does the forming of a woman from a man not demonstrate the fundamental unity and equality of human beings? Do the words 'helper' and 'suitable' denote inequality and the inadequacy of a woman? Is the Holy Spirit not a helper? Is there a relationship between the kind of 'help' mentioned here as the woman's role and that of the Holy Spirit? Who needs help, the weaker or the stronger? Does the word 'helper' imply female subordination or inferiority? If so, why is God called helper in several places in the Old Testament **(e.g. I Samuel 7:12; Psalm 121:1-2)**?

3. **Genesis 1:26-28** emphasises that male and female were created together in God's image. At that moment male and female had both equity and equality. They were equal partners in God's project. **Genesis 2:18-23** emphasises how God specifically created a woman. If Adam and Eve had not sinned, how would relations between male and female be today?

4. Read **Luke 24:1-10; Acts 2:16-18; 2 Corinthians 3:17-18; Ephesians 4:15-16, 22-24.**

> What do you find in these specific texts about the role of women and men in the Bible (first two texts) and about Christians and the image of God (last two texts)?

Conclusion

The creation story forms the foundation of our relationships with God, with one another and with creation. Male and female were together created in God's image, and both were created as special and unique physical, social and spiritual beings, intended to have relationships with one another and with God. There is no discrimination between male and female in **Genesis 1** and their mandate from God was the same for both. **Genesis 2** gives more attention to the differences between male and female and highlights what bound them together and how they complement each other. It also emphasises that a woman is an individual human being with dignity and worth and that man and woman are designed to have a fulfilling and dynamic relationship with one another.

To be created in the image of God expresses the truth that men and women have inherent value and dignity. It also implies the responsibility of being God's representatives on earth. God mandated Adam and Eve *(through what is known as the Genesis Dominion Mandate of* **Genesis 1:28***)* to rule over the earth and to care for it. When men act violently towards women, they violate persons who were created in the image of God. When we plunder the earth through environmentally unfriendly actions, we disregard our standing as representatives of God.

The four gospels agree that women played prominent roles during Jesus' earthly ministry, and at both the crucifixion and the resurrection. Women were the first to find the empty grave and to see Jesus again. They were the first messengers of the life-changing fact that Christ was alive.

In Acts, Peter interprets the outpouring of the Holy Spirit on the gathered community of Jesus' followers – men and women alike – as the fulfilment of the prophecy of Joel (**Acts 2:16-18**).

Paul describes the Christian life as a process of growing to full maturity (**Ephesians 4:15-16**) and a putting off the old self to put on the new

(Ephesians 4:22-24). This new, mature person is created to be like God **(verse 24),** and this is equally true of both men and women.

When we view the story of the fall and its consequences **(Genesis 3)** as permanently defining relationships between men and women we disregard the gospel of Jesus Christ. **Galatians 3:13a** says, *Christ has redeemed us from the curse of the law, having become a curse for us.* In Christ, we are redeemed from the curses of Genesis 3 and the law. We should note that relations between men and women are primarily defined by their mutual creation in God's image and their mutual mandate to represent God. Men and women are saved though Christ to become temples of the Holy Spirit. In Christ Jesus *there is neither male nor female* **(Galatians 3:28)**.

Jesus demonstrated what this meant in practice. Every woman who met Jesus was affirmed and enriched by Him. It is remarkable how many women Jesus healed. He released women from the cultural and religious bonds that crippled them in many ways. In no way does this detract from the way in which Jesus related to men. When we follow Jesus through the gospels, we see equal consideration for men and women.

What Jesus did was unknown and uncommon in those times and in that cultural setting. One example is the woman at the well of Samaria in *John 4*. Not only did Jesus transcend the bounds of gender, but He also looked beyond culture: it was not acceptable for Jewish men to speak to women at all, much less a Samaritan.

We need to treat every male and female with respect for they have equal value as persons. Women have value for who they are and not because they are married, have children or exhibit feminine qualities we like. Men have value for who they are and not because they demonstrate certain masculine features, are married, have children or are rich. Although Christians may appear to agree with these principles, they sometimes subscribe to the idea that women are inferior or participate in practices that oppress women. We easily succumb to views and attitudes that degrade women or objectify them. When men and women are forced to live according to gender stereotypes, we restrict their potential to become the people God created them to be.

Notes and reflections

CHAPTER 2: Our calling to honour, uphold, and restore the dignity and value of every human being

Biblical texts:

Mark 14:3-9; Deuteronomy 10:17-19; Proverbs 31:28-31; Isaiah 56:3-5; Galatians 3:26-29

Introduction

This is a true story, but the names have been changed.

Nomusa and her husband Themba Dube attended the Hem of His Garment Ministries in Nquthu in KwaZulu-Natal. Themba abused Nomusa but no one knew because Themba was wealthy and active in church activities. One day Nomusa came to her pastor, Thulasizwe Mkhize, with the request that he talk to her husband about the way he treated her. *I feel like a servant and a doormat in the way he treats me,* she sobbed. She was stunned when the man of God told her that she should be thankful to be married to such a wealthy man who was also an elder in the church and gifted in a number of ways. When Pastor Mkhize told her that according to the Bible she had to submit to her husband, she did not know how to object. After a long lecture, which Pastor Mkhize called counselling, he prayed and asked God to give Nomusa a submissive spirit so that she would never object to anything her husband wished. Why did the pastor respond in this way?

Why could he not understand Nomusa's feeling that her husband did not value her? Why could he not recognise Nomusa as a person with inherent dignity? Why could he not see that the abuse she was suffering at the hand of someone who was meant to be her equal partner was fundamentally wrong?

Mark 14:3-9 does not tell us why the woman of Bethany decided to anoint Jesus. The fact that she used her very costly ointment implies that she was overwhelmed with gratitude, but the guests were not impressed. Jesus accepted the anointing as something she did for his burial. This story is about Jesus, but it is also an important story about a woman and how men reacted to her.

Key biblical reflection points

1. Read **Mark 14:3-9** and find out how the guests reacted to this woman. Read **verses 4 and 5** again. What effect would this have had on the woman?

2. Read **verses 6, 8 and 9** and see Jesus' response to the woman and to the people's reactions. What effect would this have had on the woman?

3. How did Jesus protect her and in what way did He honour her? Would you agree that Jesus honoured, upheld and restored her dignity and value?

> **4.** Read through the following: **Deuteronomy 10:17-19; Proverbs 31:28-31; Isaiah 56:3-5; Galatians 3:26-29.** What do these scriptures teach about the dignity of people? Look at the social status and gender of the various people.

Conclusion

The story of the anointing at Bethany shows a woman who was overwhelmed with gratitude (and possibly an understanding that Jesus' life was in danger). She used her expensive ointment to anoint Jesus. Some guests angrily criticised her actions as a waste of money and even scolded her. Jesus' reaction showed beyond doubt that He approved of her and what she did. He reprimanded those who were critical and honoured her as a living symbol of true discipleship.

Jesus restored people's dignity by the way He interacted with them. Moses describes God as the impartial God *who administers justice for the fatherless and the widow,* **(Deuteronomy 10:18)** loving and caring for the vulnerable. The Hebrew phrase translated as, *God is not partial,* reminds us of a slave market where slave buyers first lifted up the face of the kneeling slaves to see if there was still vigour in

their eyes before buying; if their eyes were dull they
would

be rejected. God is not so; He accepts every person. God upholds the dignity of the people He created and is the God of the destitute, the poor and wronged. He calls His church to follow Him in this.

In **Proverbs 31** when King Lemuel's mother gave him a description of a capable or noble wife, she drew a picture of a super-woman who acted in many ways contrary to accepted gender roles of that time. Her worth was not derived from her husband or children and nothing is said of her physical appearance. However, her husband praised her, and her children honoured her.

Isaiah prophesied about a time when a person's acceptance among God's people would not depend on his or her ability to produce offspring. Paul emphatically stated that the distinctions between people on grounds of race, class or sex are no longer important when people belong to Christ Jesus. This does not imply that non-Christians do not have equal dignity: before God; every person has dignity and inherent value, regardless of their social status, gender, age, wealth or health.

The fact that all people have inherent dignity and value should be acknowledged in interactions between men and women, husbands and wives, and in parents' dealings with daughters and sons alike. This calls us to build relationships that transcend all our prejudices, cultural and gender stereotypes.

A person's dignity can be acknowledged, honoured, respected and affirmed, or it can be ignored, mocked, damaged or abused, with rudeness, violence, neglect, stigmatising, objectifying, gender stereotyping or discrimination. It is easy to damage someone's dignity and we should guard against such conduct.

The church has great power either to affirm or damage a person's dignity. We must sadly acknowledge that there are examples in the history of the church where female Christians have been humiliated and disgraced. When churches devalue women, they pave the way for gender discrimination.

All churches should defend the dignity of vulnerable people and oppose gender stereotyping, sexism and systems and traditions that disempower women and they should be the first place where a person's impaired dignity can be restored.

The golden rule of **Matthew 7:12 (NIV)**, *"So in everything, do to others what you would have them do to you, for this sums up the Law and the Prophets",* applies to our interaction with everyone we meet. We should honour and respect a person's dignity as we would want our own dignity to be respected, showing consideration for their well-being and listening to their stories and opinions. Jesus is our model of right conduct and therefore we should act towards vulnerable people as He would do. When we understand that gender roles are learned and perpetuated through cultures and traditions, we must also understand that the Bible is not prescriptive in this regard. This insight helps us to honour, uphold and restore the dignity of individuals who act in ways that seem foreign to us. In doing this, we do not necessarily accept or approve of all their actions, but we acknowledge and honour the person created in the image of God.

Notes and reflections

CHAPTER 3: Followers of Christ must model healthy gender relationships

Biblical texts:

Philippians 2:1-5; Matthew 7:12; Luke 7:36-50; Galatians 3:26-29; Ephesians 5:21-32

Introduction

The name has been changed in this example:

Rev Mbongeni Dlamini was known as a passionate preacher and visionary in the Assemblies of God in the Free State in South Africa. However, he had a shortcoming that hindered him from becoming a national leader and participating at a higher level. He could not stand it when other leaders disagreed with his views, and women in the church avoided working with him because he was known for his humiliating manner towards them. What was wrong with this powerful church leader? How was it possible that he could reach such heights as a preacher and leader but still struggle with relationships with other leaders and with women in particular? This is a sign of unbalanced spiritual development. There are Christians who grow in their personal strengths but who do not grow in their relationships. They remain immature in their inter-personal skills and emotional intelligence.

Christians who have developed in this one-sided

manner often hurt and harm many people, and they cannot bestow life and well-being on others.

Paul's letter to the Philippians is full of joy and encouragement. Although Paul was in prison while writing the letter, he demonstrated contentment and hope. It is in this letter that we see Paul's passionate commitment to Jesus Christ (1:20-21). Paul was zealous about his readers' commitment to Christ and their Christian fellowship. **Philippians 2:1-5** contains a strong appeal for true Christian fellowship, culminating in a plea to imitate Christ.

Key biblical reflection points

1. Read **Philippians 2:1-5** and list everything that contributes to Christian unity or fellowship, then list all that can spoil Christian fellowship.

2. Read the passage again and this time think specifically of fellowship and unity between men and women. What do you find in this passage (especially verse 3) that explains why fellowship between men and women may be spoiled? What do you find that will specifically help men and women to have true Christian fellowship (verses 2 and 4)?

3. The climax of Paul's argument is verse 5. How will male-female relations change if men and women both have the attitude of Jesus?

> 4. Read the following verses: **Matthew 7:12; Luke 7:36-50; Galatians 3:26-29; Ephesians 5:21-32.** What did you find in these texts that would help men and women to build better relations with the other sex?

Conclusion

Christians are disciples of Jesus Christ, who are being changed by the Holy Spirit to become more like Him. Imitating Christ has direct consequences for relationships.

In your relationships with one another, have the same mindset as Christ Jesus (**Philippians 2:5 NIV**). The practical outcome of having the 'mindset of Christ' is spelled out in verse 4: *not looking to your own interests but each of you to the interests of the others.* When we are changed to become like Jesus, we are not supposed to be jealous or proud (**verse 3**): we should be kind and compassionate (**verse 1**). We are supposed to agree with one another, love one another and work together with one mind and purpose (**verse 2**). This is how mature Christians should conduct themselves in all   relationships.

This applies to women and men since normal Christian fellowship includes both genders. **Philippians 2:1-5** is a crucial guideline for healthy, life-giving gender relations. There is an interesting similarity between Paul's words in **Philippians 2:4** and those of Jesus in **Matthew 7:12.** When we apply the principle, do to others what you would have them do to you (NIV), to our gender relations we will bestow well-being. The story in **Luke 7:36-50** is a practical demonstration of how Jesus responded in a situation where a man looked down upon a woman. He openly opposed the Pharisee's attitude and looked out for the interests of this woman. Paul's statement in **Galatians 3:26-29** removes all uncertainty about equality between male and female in Jesus Christ.

We need to read. **Ephesians 5:21-32** carefully and pay attention to Paul's directives to husbands. Here again the example of Jesus Christ is used to appeal to the husband to love his wife the way Christ loves the church. Christ gave his life for the church so that the church would be the beautiful institution that it is. In the same way a husband should sacrifice himself for his wife so that she can thrive.

Paul even quotes **Genesis 2:24** where the creation story concludes with the pronouncement that the man will be completely dedicated to his wife. Although these examples apply primarily to Christian fellowship and Christian marriage, Christian men and women should apply the principles to all their relations with the other sex. A Christian man cannot truthfully look out for the best interests of his wife and sacrifice himself for her well-being while his attitude to other women is humiliating or he uses foul language about women in male-only conversations. Christian men and women should refuse to blame or shame the other sex or to reflect the attitude that men are superior to women.

It is easy to become accustomed to long-standing attitudes and opinions. However, our Christian hope inspires us to look at relationships in our church and community and envisage new approaches that will demonstrate the love of Christ for all. We specifically need living hope when confronted with oppressive gender relations. When Paul writes about maturity in **Ephesians 4,** he uses the illustration that Christian growth is like putting off old clothes and putting on the new clothes of Christ **(4:22-24).**

To grow in Christ, we need to put off relationships that are selfish, humiliating and founded on gender stereotypes and *put on* relationships that value others above ourselves, and demonstrate caring about their well-being. Such interactions will be life-giving and will be evidenced by men and women supporting one another.

When Christian men and women encourage each other to become the people that God created them to be, they will not impose gender stereotypes. Mature Christians have healthy relationships with God and their neighbours. Maturity in Christ will help us to understand and accept that people are not all the same, and to be comfortable with differences. Mature people are happy to bless and compliment others and receive blessings and compliments. Such men and women are positive role models for younger Christians.

Notes and reflections

CHAPTER 4: Together, men and women are partners in God's diverse and inclusive family

Introduction

To visitors at the Sunday service of the Church of the Cross in Greytown in KwaZulu-Natal, the church appeared to be a vibrant place where everyone was happy to serve the Lord. However, one attentive visitor noticed that there were a few elders who kept a strict eye on everyone and everything. Even the preacher looked to these men from time to time to see if they were still approving of his message. Quite a number of women and children also looked anxiously in the direction of these elders. Some of the women, when asked about this, reported that these elders ruled the congregation with unyielding authority. While they were happy, everyone could relax, but let anyone who stepped out of line beware! The worst was when a woman or girl angered them.

What do you think of this congregation? Does it sound familiar? Even if these men who controlled the congregation meant to serve God, the question remains: could there be any real fellowship and teamwork between men and women when a few men exercised unyielding authority over the rest?

I Corinthians 12:12-27 is firstly a passage describing congregational unity where *Jews or Greeks, slaves or free* belong together. However, all New Testament references to the church assume that men, women and children belong to it. Therefore, it is enlightening to explore this passage with specific reference to the relationships between men and women.

Key biblical reflection points

1. In **1 Corinthians 12:13** Paul refers to Jews or Gentiles, slave or free. In **Galatians 3:28** he adds male and female to these examples. Read **1 Corinthians 12:12-27** and check what perspectives are opened when we apply these arguments to relations between male and female.

2. The examples of **verses 15-16** represent internalised inferiority. What does this say about how women have been brought up to feel inferior? The examples in **verse 21** represent degrading attitudes. What does this say about how men sometimes talk about women? What corrections are proposed in **verses 22-25?**

3. Read **verses 26 and 27** and see how the unity of the church as body of Christ should change relations between men and women.

> How should men and women relate and work together to serve the unity of the body of Christ?
>
> 4. Read through the following verses: **Genesis 2:18-25; Matthew 1:18-25, 2:13-15, 19-23; Luke 8:1-3; Acts 1:14, 2:4, 17-18.** What do they say about partnership between male and female?

Conclusion

In **1 Corinthians 12:12-27** Paul argues for unity and harmony where everyone, Jews and Greeks, slaves and free, (and we may add male and female) is honoured, respected and cared for. This is indeed a vision of an inclusive family of God. In God's family people from all walks of life, irrespective of their social standing (married, widowed or single), are welcome and incorporated. God creates His church in Christ so *that there should be no division in the body, but that its parts should have equal concern for each other* (**verse 25**).

Paul rejects the idea that some Christians may say to others, "*I have no need of you*". Since this is the case, a Christian man should certainly not say anything of this nature to a Christian woman. Gender stereotyping has no place in God's inclusive family.

Differences between men and women are not grounds for feelings of superiority or inferiority, or for exclusive or discriminatory attitudes, but rather should provide opportunities to complement one another.

The Hebrew text of **Genesis 2** does not support the view that men are superior to women. The word for 'helper' does not mean 'servant', but rather 'rescuer', as this word is often used to refer to God as our helper (e.g. **Psalm 146:5**). God created someone to complete Adam, to complement him and to be his partner. This story comes after the events of Genesis 1 where we learn that male and female had together received a mandate from God. Adam and Eve belonged together and together received a mandate from God. Male and female were partners with shared responsibility, task and purpose.

According to **Genesis 3,** the beautiful relationship between Adam and Eve was damaged by sin. The concepts of the superiority of men and the subjugation of women belong to **Genesis 3 and not Genesis 2.** The good news is that Jesus Christ came to rescue us from a life dominated by sin and death (**Romans 7:24, 25a**). God recreates us as new persons in

Christ to live the life that He has prepared for us **(Ephesians 2:10).**

Therefore, we have to do away with the behaviour that has its roots in **Genesis 3.** We should be renewed by the Spirit and live the new life as people created in God's image (**Ephesians 4:22-24**).

Matthew emphasises Joseph's role in the story of the birth of Jesus. Joseph was a man who did everything necessary to protect and care for Mary and the baby Jesus. Their safety was his first priority. Joseph and Mary were together responsible and worked as partners in caring for the baby.

When Jesus ministered and travelled publicly, He was accompanied by both men and women. Contrary to rabbinic teaching of the time, He taught all of them as His wider group of disciples, and contrary to the culture and customs of that time, a number of women even provided for the daily needs of Jesus and His followers (**Luke 8:1-3**). Jesus accepted them, not as extras, but as part of His group. After Jesus completed His mission and ascended to heaven, Luke draws a picture of a group where men and women together participated without discrimination, bias or prejudice. According to **Acts 1:14, 2:4, 17-18** women featured prominently before and after Pentecost.

CHAPTER 4

Peter emphasised that God's Spirit had been promised to both sons and daughters, which clearly means men and women. At Pentecost, the Holy Spirit empowered men and women alike to build the church of Jesus Christ. We need to honour the Spirit's gifts to both men and women.

Created in God's image and restored in Christ to equal standing, men and women are fellow workers or partners in God's kingdom. When men and women find their positions and roles where they contribute to the body of Christ and care for one another, they create beautiful stories and build healthy families and communities. (Read **Ruth 2** for an Old Testament example). Healthy partnerships between men and women display God's inclusive family and foster harmony where everyone is honoured, respected and cared for. We are together (male and female) called to be faithful stewards of God in caring for one another, our families, the church and the world.

Notes and reflections

CHAPTER 5: Our attitude towards people: accepting them with Christ's grace

Biblical texts:

Romans 15:7; Luke 6:36-42; Colossians 3:12-15;
Galatians 5:22-6:2; Micah 6:8; Matthew 23:23

Introduction

This is a true story, but names have been changed.

While visiting Peniel Church of God near Kranskop in KwaZulu-Natal, I heard a surprising announcement. Pastor Thabo Mazibuko announced that Sister Gertrude Sithole would not continue to lead the choir for the next twelve months because Gertrude needed time to grieve her husband Mthokozisi's death. There were some murmurs among the younger women in church, but most of the congregants seemed to accept it. Sister Gertrude's husband Mthokozisi had died a few months before. Gertrude had annoyed the elders of the Peniel Church of God when she stopped wearing black clothes within three months of her husband's death. Sister Gertrude heard about their decision with regards to the choir only when it was announced to the congregation on that Sunday morning. She had not been consulted or even informed beforehand. She was furious and walked out of the meeting, angry and humiliated.

At the next meeting of the church council they decided to discipline Sister Gertrude for her behaviour. They sent her a letter to inform her that she was under church discipline. The three counts against her were: breaking the 'church rule' about wearing black to mourn her husband for a year; continuing to sing in the choir as if nothing had happened; and walking away from a disciplinary session in church.

What happened in this congregation? Does it sound familiar? What role did cultural gender expectations (e.g. 'a widow has to wear black clothes for a year') play in the functioning of the church and the relationship between the male leaders and this prominent woman? Did the decisions of the leaders serve Christ, or did they serve their culture?

Paul spent a significant part of his letter to the **Romans** on the issue of strained relations in the congregation between 'the weak' and 'the strong' in faith (**14:1 – 15:13**). Through the centuries, there have been many reasons for disunity and even hostility between Christians, which include strained relations between men and women. Whatever the reason for conflict among Christians, there are important lessons to be learned from this part of Paul's letter. Look at Paul's concluding plea for unity in **15:1-13** and how it applies to the relationship between men and women.

Key biblical reflection points

1. Read **Romans 15:1-9** and identify Paul's case for establishing unity **(verses 5-6)**. Why is unity important **(verse 5)**? What is the outcome of unity among Christians **(verse 6)**?

2. **Verse 7** is the climax of Paul's appeal for unity. Why is this verse so important? What did Christ do to accept us? Read **Romans 5:6-10** to see how Christ accepted (welcomed) us.

3. How would you apply the appeal of **verse 7** to a situation where there are strained relations between men and women? What about a situation where someone has offended you?

4. Read **Luke 6:36-42; Colossians 3:12-15; Galatians 5:22 – 6:2; Micah 6:8; Matthew 23:23.** What do you find in these texts that helps us understand what it means to accept someone with Christ's amazing grace?

Conclusion

When Paul wrote to the church in Rome about disunity and strained relationships among them, his final argument was that they should accept one another in the same way that Jesus Christ accepted each of them.

Christ is our model and example of how we should relate to one another. In Chapter 5 Paul explained how Christ has accepted us: He died for us while we were still weak, sinners and His enemies – now this is amazing grace! When Christians look at one another with Christ's attitude and accept one another with Christ's grace, all strained relations can be overcome. It will glorify God when all join together to praise Him. Christian fellowship implies that people are mercifully accepted and embraced with the love of Christ.

According to Luke, Jesus expects His disciples to be as merciful as their Father in heaven. Jesus explains merciful conduct as refraining from judging and condemning others, forgiving offences, giving freely and not being hypocritical in the way we focus on people's shortcomings. In **Colossians 3:12-15,** Paul expands on the principle he gave in Romans 15:7. Yet again Christ is our model for forgiving each other.

Christian fellowship and unity is built on compassion, patience, forgiving and bearing with one another. The fruit of the Holy Spirit in the Christian's life **(Galatians 5:22-23)** is well known. However, do we remember that Paul immediately applies this fruit to relations between Christians? The outcome of the Holy Spirit's work in a Christian cannot be superiority or pride, but rather the willingness to stand alongside someone who has stumbled. To accept someone in Christ is to embrace that person with Christ's love, to help carry his or her burdens and to correct him or her gently if necessary.

When we accept Christ's amazing grace, we act according to the core principles of God's Law. These are to love God and our neighbour with conduct that is merciful and humble. However, according to **Micah 6:8 and Matthew 23:23,** mercy and faith are always accompanied by justice. Therefore, we have the responsibility to ensure that our action towards one individual does not result in injustice to another. This is particularly relevant when a person has acted wrongfully against another. For example, if a man has humiliated a woman in public or in the church, both the man and the woman have to be accepted, but the woman must receive justice.

To accept someone with Christ's amazing grace is not a call for limitless tolerance. The issues Paul addresses in **Romans 14:1 – 15:13** are not 'essential' salvation matters. When salvation through

faith in Jesus Christ alone was at stake, Paul did not
hesitate to

challenge the Apostle Peter in public (see **Galatians 2:11-16**). In the passage preceding **Colossians 3:12-15**, Paul warns against sinful actions. **Galatians 6:1** is about the restoration of someone who has fallen into sin. In **Luke 6:42** Jesus instructs his disciples to take out the log in their own eyes so that they can help their neighbour with the speck in his or her eye. To accept someone should not be to sacrifice justice or 'essential' salvation matters.

Acceptance includes the person who has been sinned against (for example, a woman who has been abused) as well as the sinner (the abuser). Both need support and restoration, but their paths towards restoration will be different. A rapist must be reported to the police and the church should not seek to cover up the incident. The victim should be in a position to decide on the way forward and what actions should be taken, without fear of reprisal or victimisation by the church. The victim should be confident of the church's support and full protection.

Grace, mercy and kindness are always accompanied by justice and caring for the vulnerable. The abused woman will need healing and grace to forgive, while the abuser needs compassionate help to obey God in future. Restoration of the abuser does not depend on public confession, but there should be personal confession and penitence. During this process the church must take the protection of the woman into consideration.

Christians and the church are called to accept people and embrace them with understanding, to support them and to walk with them. Accepting people should not depend on a person's status, gender, age, wealth or health. When gender stereotyping excludes people, we contradict Christ's love.

Notes and reflections

____

____

____

____

____

____

____

____

____

CHAPTER 6: Our duty to minister healing and restoration, to protect the vulnerable and oppose violence

Biblical texts:

Isaiah 1:15-17; Psalm 82:2-4; Genesis 3:16-19; Romans 5:17-18; Exodus 3:9-10; Colossians 3:17 – 4:1

Introduction

After Pastor Mkhize told Nomusa she had to submit to her husband Themba and prayed for a submissive spirit in her, she went home with a heavy heart. On her way home she decided that she had no choice but to try her best to do what her husband approved of. For a few days nothing serious happened. However, the next Sunday after the service, Pastor Mkhize talked to Themba and told him about Nomusa's visit and complaints. He assured Themba that he did not really believe her complaints and had encouraged her to submit to him. Themba came home enraged and when Nomusa tried to explain why she went to the pastor he lost his temper and assaulted her physically.

What happened in this story? What contributed to the situation that led to the violence Nomusa experienced? What should happen next?

Isaiah 1:2-20 has the structure of a lawsuit. God brings Israel to court and accuses His nation of rebellion before the witnesses of heaven and earth (**verse 2**). More accusations are added in **verses 3 and 4**. In **verses 10-17** God responds to the objection from Israel that they cannot be guilty since they have fulfilled their religious duties. However, God argues that they cannot hide injustice underneath religious activities **(15-17)**. The surprise is that at this point of proven guilt, God offers forgiveness **(18-20)**. Although **verse 18** is so beautiful, we need to listen to the serious words in the previous verses.

Key biblical reflection points

1. Read **Isaiah 1:15-17**. According to **verses 11-14** all the religious activities of Israel were in vain. **Verses 15 and 17** indicate what the problem was. Also read **Isaiah 1:23, 3:14-15 and 5:7-8** and find out why God is so disappointed with Israel.

2. The only reference to women is to widows. However, you can imagine what women experienced when men's 'hands are full of blood' **(1:15)**, princes ignore the widow **(1:23)**, elders and princes devour vineyards and crush people **(3:14-15)** and there is bloodshed and cries among the people **(5:7)**.

3. God promises forgiveness **(1:18)** but He expects new life. What are His expectations according to **verse 17?** The church cannot be seen as being 'soft' on criminality. Gender-based violence is a criminal offence.

4. Read the following verses: **Psalm 82:2-4; Exodus 3:9-10; Colossians 3:17 – 4:1.** What do you discover about God's expectations of his children? Read also **Genesis 3:16-19 and Romans 5:17-18** and see how Jesus Christ turned the situation of **Genesis 3** around.

Conclusion

When we read that God turns his eyes away from outstretched hands of prayer with blood on them, we are reminded of many other passages in the Bible that tell that God hates violence (see **Exodus 20:13; Deuteronomy 27:24-25; Psalm 11:5; Proverbs 6:16-17; Matthew 5:21-22, 38-44; Romans 12:18-21**).

In the lawsuit of **Isaiah 1** God accuses his people of many injustices, including violence. When injustices are the order of the day in a community, the vulnerable (for example women and children) are the first to suffer. When violence becomes 'normal', it becomes easy for men to use violence, even against their own family members. **Psalm 82:2-4** declares that God expects people in authority to serve justice and peace, protect the weak and act humanely. They must rescue the weak from the hand of the wicked (verse 4). When God called Moses, He said that He saw the oppression of his people and heard their cries. God sees and hears when women are oppressed.

A careful reading of **Colossians 3:17 – 4:1 (NRSV)** shows that although Paul asks married women, children and slaves to behave according to their different social standings, it is the men who are reminded three times (as husbands, fathers and masters) not to misuse their positions of authority. The directives, never treat them harshly, do not provoke your children and treat your slaves justly and fairly are clearly meant to restrain men. The passage stands between the call of **3:17** to do everything in the name of the Lord Jesus and the reminder of **4:1** that everyone, including men, must submit to Christ. When verses from this passage are used to defend men's domination over women, it is contrary to the intention of the whole passage and constitutes selective reading. The Bible does not give anyone unconditional power since human authority is always subject to the final authority of the risen Christ (**Colossians 2:10**).

The story of Genesis 3 is also used by some to support their view that women are supposed to suffer. This way of thinking disregards Paul's teaching in *Romans 5* that not only points the finger at Adam for our world's sinful state, but also declares that Jesus Christ turned the situation around.

Adam brought sin and death, but Christ brought abundance of grace and the gift of righteousness *(verse 17)* and justification of life *(verse 18)*. Christians should live in the light of ***Romans 5 and not Genesis 3.***

Jesus expected His disciples to be peacemakers and taught them to respond in non-violent ways to violence (read *Matthew 5:9)*. The church cannot stay impartial where gender-based violence occurs, but should minister reconciliation, healing and restoration. The Bible's passion for justice and the biblical vision of the just king motivate the church to mediate on behalf of victims of violence.

The church must speak out against all forms of violence, especially violence used by the powerful against the weak, which is a most blatant form of injustice. A husband who acts violently against his wife violates the clear instruction of the Bible to treat her with respect **(1 Peter 3:7)**. The church should firstly promote non-violent responses to violence, and we must protect individuals who are in abusive relationships and never underestimate the harm done by such violence. When gender-based violence is prevalent in a marriage the only solution may be for the wife to be separated from her husband.

The Bible shows that when people in authority reject God's rule (justice), Christians are not bound by their conscience to submit to them **(Daniel 3:16-18, 6:10-11; Acts 4:19, 5:29).** However, this decision should not be taken easily and only after consulting with other Christians. Violence in a marriage denies the very basis of marriage for it negates love and trust and truthfulness. The church should not give up hope of ministering to a violent person (while ensuring the safety and support of the victim) and succeeding in the aim of saving a marriage. The Holy Spirit helps Christians overcome their violent inclinations, but this may not be a promise that the perpetrator can immediately succeed in keeping and restoring a violent person may involve a long journey.

Notes and reflections

CHAPTER 7: Our ministry as servant leaders who share responsibilities

Biblical texts:
Luke 22:24-27; Matthew 1:18-25, 2:13-15, 19-23; Luke 10:38-42; John 13:12-17; Philippians 2:1-5

Introduction

When Pastor Nyiko Maluleke from Giyani was chosen at the national assembly to be the leader of the Apostolic Faith Church there was disagreement among the members. While some were happy to have someone, they respected as a devoted Christian, others thought that he was too modest and soft-spoken. The newspapers used this as something of a sensation and ran stories that the Apostolic Faith Church was in trouble because it chose a powerless man to lead them in a time of disunity.

What is your reaction to this story? Do you think churches need strong and powerful leaders that can unite the church with charismatic guidance? Is there an opportunity in the church for leaders who demonstrate the fruit of the Spirit: for example, patience, kindness and humility?

We read several times in the gospels that Jesus' disciples quarrelled about which one was the greatest. This confirms our own experience that

there are many people with a strong need to exercise
greater

authority. The fact that we see the same thing among Christians and in churches raises the question as to how we implement Jesus' warnings against seeking authority.

Key biblical reflection points

1. Read **Luke 22:24-27** and see how Jesus was disappointed with his disciples. This was not the first incident (see **Luke 9:46-48**). Why did the disciples struggle with the principle of who is the greatest?

2. Although Jesus responds with patience, He reprimands them in no uncertain terms. What is the essence of His teaching on authority among his followers (compare **Matthew 18:1-4**)?

3. Read **Luke 22:24-27** again and note the significance of how Jesus uses Himself as the right example. Describe how Jesus modelled leadership.

4. Read **Matthew 1:18-25.** What examples of men and women playing important roles (first two verses) and about servant leadership (last two verses) do you find? For more examples of important roles and servant leadership, read **Matthew 2:13-15, 19-23; Luke 10:38-42; John 13:12-17; Philippians 2:1-5.**

Conclusion

Jesus' teaching about authority and leadership among His followers is recorded in all four gospels. He warned them not to follow the examples of authority and power they saw in the world around them. Jesus modelled the role of a leader who serves. Although He had all power and authority, He washed his disciples' feet, a job that was normally done by a slave (see **John 13**). He laid down his life for them (and us) when He died on the cross. Jesus' appeal to his disciples to follow His example is echoed in Paul's appeal that believers should have the same mindset as Jesus and demonstrate this by unselfish behaviour, prioritising the interests of others **(Philippians 2:1-5)**. Church leaders need to show this attitude in all they do and in all their relationships.

The gospel of Matthew opens with the nativity story and underlines the role of Joseph. This man, who was the earthly father to the boy Jesus, was willing to follow all God's instructions and gave his all for the well-being and safety of Mary and her child.

He and Mary together were the parents who cared for Jesus as a baby and throughout His boyhood. The disciples of Jesus were the people whom He trained to become leaders in His church. Luke tells us (**Luke 10: 38-42**) that there was an argument between the sisters Martha and Mary when Mary chose to sit down among Jesus' disciples. Jesus protected Mary against Martha's anger and explained that her choice to do something that was contrary to their customs and her sister's expectations was actually a good decision. To sit at the Lord's feet and listen to what he was saying (**verse 39**) defined Mary as a disciple of Jesus. In accepting her as such and protecting her, Jesus also acted contrary to their culture and specifically contrary to the behaviour of rabbis of the time. It was unthinkable for them to have women as disciples. There were many women who followed Jesus as disciples and whom He accepted alongside the twelve.

During the events leading up to and surrounding Jesus' crucifixion, at His resurrection and ascension, as well as at Pentecost, women were prominent observers and participants (**Matthew 27:55**).

They were the first to witness the empty grave, to meet Jesus and to proclaim the message that Christ is risen (**Luke 24:1-12**). After His resurrection, women, including His mother, played important roles (**Acts 1:14**). Women continued to contribute significantly in the early congregations (**Acts 18:26; Romans 16:3-15**). This is also in line with Old Testament records concerning women whose lives had great significance: for example, Naomi, Hannah (wife of Elkanah), Abigail (Nabal's wife) and the unnamed woman of **Proverbs 31:10-31.**

The birth of the church reminds us of the birth of humankind. Just as male and female were together mandated in Genesis 1 to represent God, so the Holy Spirit empowered both men and women to constitute the body of Christ (God's representatives). The stories of Jesus' ministry and of the earliest congregations show the involvement of women such as was unknown in the patriarchal cultures of those times. In Christ they were restored to be part of God's kingdom of priests (**Romans 5:17; Revelation 5:9-10**). This forms the context for interpreting verses that speak of restrictions on women.

The outpouring of the Holy Spirit at Pentecost fulfilled Joel's prophecy that God would pour out His Spirit on sons and daughters, men and women (**Acts 2:16-18**). New life in Christ is given to both men and women. The Spirit bears fruit in both men and women. The 'wisdom from heaven' is given to both men and women. The Holy Spirit bestows gifts on both men and women. Spiritual leadership should be recognised in those who are spiritually mature and gifted with no restrictions as to gender. When we exclude women from leadership roles and exempt men from servant roles, we diminish the capacity of the church. Since one of the important metaphors for the church in the New Testament is 'the bride of Christ', it is reasonable to acknowledge that women will take up their appropriate and equal standing in the church.

Notes and reflections

CHAPTER 8: Searching for solutions with wisdom from the Holy Spirit

> **Biblical texts:**
> *James 3:13-18; Proverbs 31:10-31; Acts 18:24-28;*
> *Romans 12:1-2; Ephesians 5:15-21*

Introduction

This book on breaking the silence on gender matters in the church touches on many difficult and sensitive issues. For a long time, the church has avoided this discussion. However, the wise person is the one who prays for guidance from the Holy Spirit on such matters and seeks counsel in God's Word with a teachable spirit, rather than opposing everything that does not align with their preconceived ideas. A wise person will listen to their peers, including people from the opposite sex, with an open mind and heart, hoping to grow their own understanding. This will help them realise what God's will means in practice. Wisdom is not knowledge about a theory; the aim of wisdom is to do the right thing at the right time.

When it comes to wisdom, men and women are alike, since we all need wisdom as a gift from God in order to be the people God created us to be and to promote a deeper understanding of gender, thus bridging divisions between male and female.

The letter of James was written to a church under such pressure that it seemed as if it would result in divisions and factions. James pleaded with them rather to stay united by following the example and teaching of Jesus. In **chapter 3,** he contrasted the wise person who was able to make peace and harvest righteousness or justice **(3:18)** with the person with a careless tongue and earthly wisdom who would bring disorder **(3:16).** Pray for heavenly wisdom, was James' plea.

Key biblical reflection points

1. Read **James 3:14-16** and identify the characteristics of false wisdom. Note that **verse 14** describes the person, verse 15 refers to the origin, and **verse 16** explains the consequences.

2. Read **James 3:13, 17-18** and find out the 'roots', 'branches' and 'fruits' of wisdom that come from the Holy Spirit, which is the wisdom from above.

3. In **verses 17-18** James lists the characteristics of true wisdom. Consult different translations and describe each 'fruit' in your own words and in your own home language. Can these characteristics be divided into two groups – those that seem to be more feminine and those that seem to be more masculine? What do you realise when you try to do this?

> **4.** Read through one of the following: **Proverbs 31:10-31; Acts 18:24-28; Romans 12:1-2; Ephesians 5:15-21.** Pay special attention when there are references in the text to male or female. What do you find out about wisdom in theses passages of scripture?

Conclusion

Gender confronts us with complex issues, deeply rooted in church and cultural traditions and associated with people with power and influence. We therefore need wisdom from the Holy Spirit, to build relations between men and women that can stand the test of justice and bring peace. Wisdom is not gender specific; its characteristics are sometimes feminine and sometimes masculine. This is also true of the fruit of the Spirit in **Galatians 5:22-23.** Wisdom from the Holy Spirit will help us understand the complex issues of gender, the needs of people struggling with gender stereotypes and the burdens of vulnerable people. We need wise men and wise women to build good partnerships between male and female.

Proverbs, the book of wisdom, concludes with a powerful description of the capable wife who is (among all her wonderful qualities) a wise woman **(Proverbs 31:26).** It is sometimes difficult to distinguish when Proverbs describes wisdom as a woman and when it refers to a woman who is wise.

Apollos was a powerful preacher in the early church. In Corinth, some even preferred him above the Apostle Paul. But Apollos would not have reached such heights were it not for Priscilla and Aquila. They were both well known to Paul and had travelled with him. **Acts 18:24-28** shows how this woman and her husband (she is mentioned first and in **1 Corinthians 16:19** alone) gave this up-coming preacher 'master classes' in theology, so that he developed into one of the best preachers of the early church.

Paul's appeal in **Romans 12:1-2,** to be transformed by the renewing of your minds, so that you may discern what is the will of God (NRSV) is directed to a congregation of both men and women. The church cannot afford men or women who are set in their ways and unwilling to be transformed.

There is a particular danger when we value our culture and traditions above God's kingdom. Paul's well-known appeal to be filled with the Spirit (**Ephesians 5:18**) leads up to his instructions to married women and men (**verses 21-32**). Spirit-filled Christians sing psalms and songs (**verse 19**), thank God at all times and for everything (**verse 20**) and exercise mutual submission (**verse 21**).

God urges us to seek wisdom and promises to give it. The Bible is our treasury of wisdom and the teachings of our church will also assist us in our search for wise understanding. However, we must also listen attentively and without prejudice to the stories, views and insight of people who may be different from us, either in gender or in their traditional gender roles. Only when we are willing to listen and learn from one another will we grow in wisdom.

A teachable mindset and humble seeking for insight should accompany our prayers for wisdom from the Holy Spirit. The Spirit will guide us to determine what is right and good and help us to act accordingly.

When we face dysfunctional relationships between men and women, we need wisdom to address gender issues in sensitive and responsible ways that empower vulnerable people. Wisdom will guide us to deal responsibly with issues of human sexuality, gender roles and sexual orientation. We have to be open to the complexity of situations and problems and guard against simplistic responses that do not solve complex situations, but instead antagonise powerful people and disempower the vulnerable.

We need wisdom to determine our own gender roles and find ways to express them, while building healthy, life-giving gender relationships.

Notes and reflections

CHAPTER 9: Breaking the silence by speaking the truth in love

Introduction

In these days of social media, difficult and traumatic situations can arise. Imagine someone taking a humiliating photograph of you that would embarrass you if others saw it. You ask the person to destroy the picture, but the next day you discover that the person has published it without your approval on platforms such as Facebook, Twitter or the like. How would you feel? What would your reactions be?

A photograph, unless it has been 'photo-shopped' represents the truth of the image in it. However, to be confronted with a humiliating picture of yourself in public can be a painful experience. Likewise, to confront someone bluntly with the truth can hurt them, damage relationships and prevent them from seeing the love of Christ in your life. We have to be careful how we speak the truth.

The primary Bible text for this Chapter is **Ephesians 4:14-15,** but we are also looking at a story from Luke's gospel that serves as a practical example for

our consideration. The story is about two men, and a woman who conducted herself in a way that was not culturally acceptable.

Key biblical reflection points

1. Read **Luke 7:36-50** and note how the Pharisee (Simon) and Jesus responded to this uninvited guest. What did the woman do that could have upset Simon?

2. Observe from the scripture Simon's view of the woman and her actions, and his attitude towards her **(verse 39)**. How does this affect his attitude towards Jesus, another man?

3. Consider Jesus' view of the woman and her actions and his attitude towards her **(verse 40-48)**. How does Jesus communicate his view to Simon? Could we say that Jesus spoke the truth in love?

4. Read through the following: **Ephesians 4:14-15; 1 Samuel 1:9-17; 2 Samuel 12:1-14 and Galatians 2:11-16.** What do you find about speaking the truth in these passages?

Conclusion

When a woman gatecrashed the dinner a Pharisee had arranged for his invited guests, the Pharisee condemned her. It is possible that he controlled his

anger to save face before his guests, but Jesus spoke up
on behalf of

the woman. He invited Simon to really look at her and to see her deep gratitude. She might have transgressed society's customs regarding formal meals, but Jesus was not offended by this. He saw her heart. We do not know what sins she had committed before this day, but we know that Jesus forgave her.

There are some interesting resemblances between this story and the story of Hannah's praying in the temple at Shiloh. Eli, the priest, made his own assumptions, judged her and reprimanded her, but Hannah insisted that the truth be told. The truth convinced Eli and he blessed her. Hannah's boldness to speak the truth in a respectful manner and Eli's willingness to listen to her story led to a wonderful blessing on her life. When the Lord sent Nathan to King David, he had the daunting task of confronting the mighty king of Israel about committing adultery and murder. Nathan spoke to David in a way that forced him to listen and opened his eyes to the injustice of his own deeds. David was willing to listen and acknowledge his guilt. Nathan's diplomacy played a crucial role. Nathan must have respected his king but was still willing to speak the truth to him.

When we read Paul's description of the day, he had to confront the Apostle Peter for separating himself from Gentile Christians, our impression is that love was not Paul's primary motivation **(Galatians 2:11-16)**. He seemed upset, and disappointed in Peter. However, although he argued with Peter, he identified himself with him as a fellow Jew who came to faith in Jesus **(verses 15-16)**. Paul did not lose his temper while speaking the truth. The repetition of the inclusive 'we' in these verses show that he embraced Peter.

Our experience with gender matters in the church may sometimes resemble these Bible passages. We might have to look again, like Simon the Pharisee, or listen with an open mind, like Eli, or even accept confrontation, like Simon Peter. Along the way we will discover many truths about gender issues and how they impact the lives of men and women in the church and in the broader society. Before we can speak the truth, we should be open to new learning and insights. We should be willing to add truth to truth and be willing to unlearn certain things.

This will, in turn, put us in positions resembling the events outlined in these Bible passages. We might, like Jesus, have to speak on behalf of a woman, or speak up for ourselves, like Hannah, or confront someone in authority, as Nathan and Paul did.

Truth hurts and damages when used as a weapon. Truth can also hurt when it is hastily spoken before someone is prepared to hear it, or when there is no emotional support for the hearer. Another destructive use of the truth is when it is applied selectively and out of context. The aim of truth spoken in love is to help people to: grow, give life, support, serve justice, and seek the Kingdom of God and to work for God's shalom.

It takes a high degree of maturity as well as courage to speak the truth in love. We need to respect people and the community in order to build better relations. Therefore, whatever the truth, it should be communicated in a sensitive, empathetic and caring way. God wants wholeness for people and therefore truth cannot simply be a matter of being right or wrong.

Fear should not prevent us from speaking the truth in love. When we keep silent, we may be withholding important truths from an individual or a community. To hide the truth can even make us accomplices of injustice. However, there are situations where it may be better to withhold the truth for the time being; for example, when we know someone will react violently to information.

One area that specifically challenges the church and faith leaders to speak out and speak the truth, is that of gender, gender stereotypes and gender-based violence. Here we need to communicate biblical truths about violence, including its effects, vulnerability and women's dignity. We should not yield to the pressure of taboos and hide the truth. We should engage with cultural practices and challenge misinterpretation of scriptures that are used to further discrimination against and oppression of women and girls.

Christian leaders are challenged to take a bold stand against attitudes and practices that negatively affect women, firstly in the church and then in our communities. Gender issues should be spoken about in public so that they become collective community social concerns.

Notes and reflections

CHAPTER 10: Called to stand up for justice

Biblical texts:
*Psalm 72:12-14; Exodus 32:9-14; Jeremiah 22:15-16;
Amos 5:14-15, 24; 1 Timothy 2:1-4*

Introduction

From an early age children develop a sense of what is fair and unfair. A young child will experience unfairness when the parents spoil a sibling and neglect them. Not all adults are similarly aware of justice and injustice: our sense of right and wrong can be numbed as we grow up. However, people who experience injustice will usually be aware that they have been wronged.

Justice is an important subject in the Bible, though it is not often discussed. God loves justice (**Psalm 37:28, Isaiah 61:8**). He is often portrayed as the One who acts justly and who brings justice to the world (**Psalm 146:6-10**), therefore His people are to imitate God in doing justice (**Amos 5:24, Micah 6:8, Zechariah 8:16-17**). Doing justice entails caring for the poor, the weak and the oppressed (**Deuteronomy 10:16-19, 24:17-18**). When Jesus started His public ministry, He identified Himself as the implementer of the justice that the prophets of the Old Testament had proclaimed (**Luke 4:18-19, 21**).

As disciples of Christ we have to be passionate about justice and stand up for it when necessary. While some people claim that our understanding of human rights (including women's and children's rights) is a recent development in history, the Old Testament already contained a vision for justice. The law of God given to Moses was meant to create a just society in Israel and the prophets advocated for justice when Israel abandoned this law. The books of wisdom such as Proverbs, Ecclesiastes and Psalms show the importance of justice for the people of God. **Psalm 72** is a good example of this vision of justice.

Key biblical reflection points

1. Read **Psalm 72:1-4, 12-14** and describe the vision of justice in this Psalm in your own words. What role should prayer play in our advocacy for justice?

2. Read **Psalm 72:12-14** again and make notes on our responsibility to advocate on behalf of the poor and the needy before those who have power and wealth.

3. There is no mention of male and female in this passage. What principles are there in this passage for our advocacy in the gender context?

> **4.** Read through the following verses: **Exodus 32:9-14; 1 Timothy 2:1-4; Jeremiah 22:15-16; Amos 5:14-15, 24.** What do you find regarding the role of God's people in bringing about justice? Note that the first two passages speak of the role of our prayers and the last two about people acting for justice.

Conclusion

Psalm 72 gives a vision of justice that challenges our ideas of a just society and of good governance. It is also an example of a fervent prayer that God will bless and use the king. We have a responsibility to pray for those who govern. This is confirmed in Paul's first letter to Timothy. The instruction to pray for all who are in authority was given at a time when Christians were a small minority and often persecuted by people in authority. **Psalm 72** is also an instruction to all who are in any position of power to act justly on behalf of the vulnerable (see also **Psalm 82:3-4**). In **Jeremiah 22** the prophet reminds those in authority that the only true and legitimate use of power is when they serve justice and care for the vulnerable **(verses 15-16).** When leaders do not serve justice, they are no longer leaders in God's eyes.

The priests of the Old Testament were responsible for the sacrificial services at the Tabernacle and in the Temple. This was essentially an intercessory ministry on behalf of the people. When other people prayed to God on behalf of someone else, they also fulfilled a priestly function.

When Moses prayed to God to forgive Israel's sins, he stood between them and destruction. He pleaded to God for mercy and his prayer was answered (**Exodus 32**). Jesus Christ is our High Priest who has taken away our sins and who intercedes for us (**Hebrews 7:24-25, 9:24**). When we pray to God on behalf of our communities and their leaders, we also fulfil a priestly ministry. This is where our advocacy starts. Our prayers for our governments and our prayers on behalf of people who suffer are an essential starting point that should be followed up with action.

The prophets of God had an acute awareness of justice and injustice. Driven by their sensitivity towards suffering and the dangers faced by vulnerable people, the prophets stood up against the rich and powerful who exploited the defenceless. **Amos 5:14-15, 24** is an example of how these prophets stood up for justice and confronted those in authority as well as the whole nation. When we stand in the gap for vulnerable and suffering people, we fulfil a prophetic function.

When we exercise advocacy through our prayers on behalf of people, and through standing in the gap for those who cannot speak for themselves, we seek justice and work for real change. This work is often done in the public sphere, but it may also entail confronting people in person, for example where men have acted violently against women. Churches need to speak up for the rights of women and girls who cannot speak for themselves or whose voices have been silenced. When the church advocates in the public sphere it will have to collaborate with other organisations, sharing in open discussion on gender issues during conferences and on other special platforms.

Advocacy includes standing up against religious, cultural and community norms and practices that are harmful or discriminatory, which means we must approach people in influential positions about healthy gender roles and gender-based violence. Advocating on behalf of people who suffer asks for courageous interaction with leaders, challenging them to serve justice.

It is not only about changing policies and getting legal action underway; at a local level it challenges everyone in our communities to actively listen to women and girls and to act with respect towards them. Without a change of attitude and behaviour in our communities, new policies will have little effect. Advocacy for the rightful place of women in society and affirming their dignity must be a priority.

Advocacy that stands up for justice must also be well planned, and needs to prioritise relevant issues, focusing on those that affect the vulnerable more severely. Advocacy will meet resistance and we need to be innovative in the way we go about it. We need to know the key moments when we can advocate and be heard and use language that will have the required impact.

Notes and reflections

BIBLIOGRAPHY

Bauckham, R 2002. *Gospel Women: Studies of the Named Women in the Gospels.* Grand Rapids: Eerdmans

Channels of Hope for Gender (COH) 2015: World Vision International Materials (unpublished)

Epp, EJ 2005. *Junia: The First Woman Apostle.* Minneapolis: Fortress Press

Fee, GD 2014. *The First Epistle to the Corinthians (NICNT).* Grand Rapids: Eerdmans

Heines-Eitzen, K 2012. *The Gendered Palimpsest: Women, Writing, and Representation in Early Christianity.* New York: Oxford

Payne, PB 2009. *Man and Woman, One in Christ: An Exegetical and Theological Study of Paul's Letters.* Grand Rapids: Zondervan

Schreiner, TR 2010. 'Philip Payne on Familiar Ground: A Review of Philip B. Payne, Man and Woman, One in Christ: An Exegetical and Theological Study of Paul's Letters' *Journal of Biblical Manhood and Womanhood* (Spring 2010): 33-46, 35

Spencer, AB 1985, *Beyond the Curse: Women called to Ministry.* Grand Rapids: Baker

OTHER BOOKS BY STANLEY MAPHOSA

Christianity 101: Understanding the First Principles of the Oracles of God

Christianity 102: Practicing the Key Principles of a Christian Life

Leadership in Principle and Practice.

Notes and reflections

Notes and reflections

Notes and reflections

Notes and reflections

Notes and reflections

Notes and reflections

Notes and reflections